Green Turtles

by Rachel Russ

OXFORD
UNIVERSITY PRESS

Egg to Adult

Green turtles are incredible animals.

This book tracks a turtle from egg to adult.

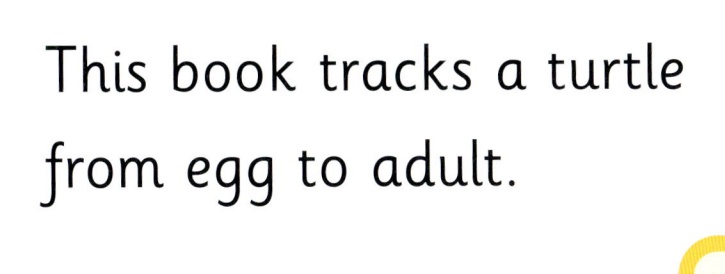

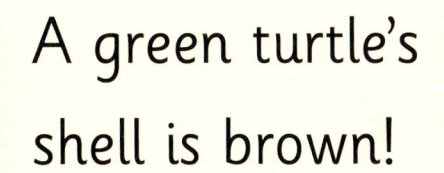

A green turtle's shell is brown!

Egg

A green turtle starts as an egg.

egg tooth

The turtle cracks its shell with an egg tooth.

The turtle gets out of the egg. It struggles to the top of the nest.

Setting Out

The turtle needs to get to the water.

There are a lot of risks.

Crabs sit and wait.

Gulls hover in the air.

The little turtle shuffles across the sand.
It has to be quick to avoid the risks.

It looks out for big fish. They lurk in the water.

Getting Bigger

The turtle hunts for snails and shrimps. It must keep feeding and getting bigger.

Turtles float far from the coast for several years.

Adult Turtle

Then the turtle swims to the coast.

Adult turtles feed on plants.

Back to the Start

The turtle is back! It started in this spot as an egg.

The turtle digs a nest for its eggs. It kicks sand on them. The eggs are hidden.

Soon, the eggs will crack. Then little turtles will pop out. They will travel like their mum.

Egg to Adult

Encourage the child to use the pictures to explain the life cycle of a green turtle.